D0054171

The Colors of Time

By Florence Jacobs

Illustrated by David Welty

👑 Hallmark Crown Editions

First appeared in *New England Galaxy* Magazine as "Album of Color Shots."
Copyright ©1972 by Hallmark Cards, Inc.,
Kansas City, Missouri. All Rights Reserved.
Printed in the United States of America.
Library of Congress Catalog Card Number: 70-168971.
Standard Book Number: 87529-240-2.

Out of a January sky star flakes begin to fall...

...gently, windlessly...

...insubstantial as frost when they pass the pane...

...ten minutes later outlining the firs

with heavy strokes of white chalk.

Catch a flake on your sleeve

and see the ultimate in design.

Lift your face...

...be lost in infinity

exploring the white world

flowing endlessly

overhead.

Time of meditation...

...when days curl closer to each other

seeking shelter from the cold

   and the darkness...

      ...shortening the very life of February.

`But in the frosted silence
the heart of the year beats stronger...

...stronger...

...and there is a feeling of expectancy...

...of urgency

that even the barren earth cannot deny.

Movement everywhere, aggressive, restless...

thrusting forward its fierce purpose

...and not to be blocked or repressed .

The clouds of March scud across the sun.

Wild eddies scoop up dead leaves...

...bite into the last bedraggled snowdrifts.

the pond is dark...

and wild with new freedom.

A strong new tide of life itself...

...beating along the gale...

...swelling in the waves...

exultation which is the forerunner

of all creation...

...all birth!

April brings a new-minted moment
that we can save
        to spend throughout the year.
The ancient willow hanging above the brook
is newly leaved into sulphur-colored mist...

...there is a low sun in the west
reaching long fingers across...
...kindling little puffs of green flame
all through the branches...
..and a storm rolling blue-black thunderheads
as an awesome backdrop in the east.

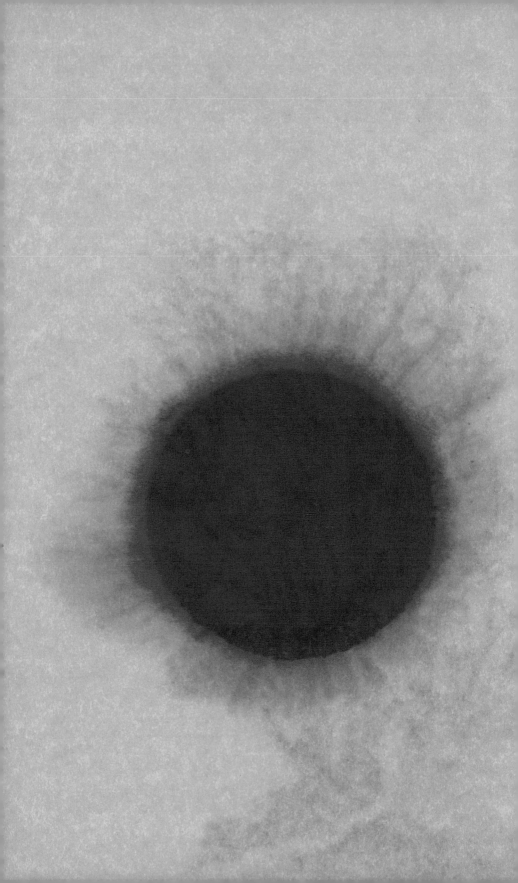

This May morning carved ivory petals

of each narcissus...

...ivory satin trunks of the birches...

...sunbeams glinting from coppery leaves...

...a yellow warbler swinging on a low bough.

Stand by the sundial.

Gaze at the triangle of massed tulips

until you are sated with glory.

Mount the low wall for a new perspective...

the shimmer, through half-closed lids,

of a rainbow brilliance.

Kneel and cup a butter-yellow blossom...

...and touch helps bear the weight of beauty

too much for sight alone.

A green tide has risen...risen...

washed over meadow and hedge...

    ...flooded to the tops of the elms.

    Here runs the whole sequence...

...blades of the June grass...

    ...pale-misted willows, delicate poplars

...somber dark plumes on the spruce row

...pool already brimmed with even-shade.

Frogs pipe a mellow motif.

Swallows draw their wide circles...

...a moon fingers the water.

There is no more breeze

than

ruffles the highest leaf.

A night touched with unearthly magic...

...the true Midsummer Eve.

July is a summer kitchen...

...fragrant

...delicious

in its raspberry jam heat.

It is a summer place

drawing us out of doors

to bask

like a contented cat,

drowsy with the sun.

Yellow myrtle

frames the stone square atop the well.

A dragonfly is like

an emerald suspended

in the stillness.

July air

is brilliant and dry and good!

Heat

soaks into the marrow

and peace

into the mind.

Along in August comes a windless morning
holding its breath
to catch earth's strong heartbeat.

　Even the aspens cease their perpetual tremor.
There is a hush...

　...a waiting for one leaf to fall
and lay bare that secret pulse.

Green is again the keynote...

but not June's fresh tones.

These are older, more sophisticated...

shading into gray rather than spring yellow.

The road winds uphill in its tunnel of elms...

every detail exaggerated...

...cool

...shadowy

...mysterious.

All this September afternoon the lake lay
under its blue haze...

a milk opal scarred now and then by the silver line
of a swift passage.

Now evening, and the lake
becomes a moonstone...

...without chop or swell

to break the frosted surface.

No lights along the shore...

cottagers have fastened their shutters

and gone away for the season.

But the deserted lake is never lonely.

Its own rich life has come back.

The diffused starshine is alive

with wings...

...and calls.

Loons' eerie laughter

echoes in every cove.

From the Point

an owl booms his five measured notes.

Suppertime now,

but who can shut the door

　　　on a single precious moment?

　　　　　Not many more such evenings!

The apple-green sunset may mean frost...

　　　...its faint lilac tinge

certainly means October.

Turn slowly...

...as afterglow streams up the west...

...darts pink tongues into the east

...flames chrome, madder, grape...

fades to soft rose.

The hunter's moon, full tonight,

climbs through a sky

just this second turned steel blue.

Satisfied, you can go in.

November nuances...

...see the subtle shades of bark...

...how many grays...

...what an opulence of browns!

It is a time of patterns...

and the pure beauty of structure is free

of the distraction of brilliant patterns...

...delicate tracing along stout willow trunk

...interlaced branches on the elm.

Follow a wood path...

unhampered by so much as an armful of bittersweet...

...unhindered by a body, even,

so light does it seem in this rare current.

Walk on through December

and into the new year...

...carrying only your memories

...and your dreams.

This book was designed and illustrated by David Welty.
The artist's unique style is the result of
experimental techniques of silk screen printing.
The typeface is Missouri, an upright calligraphic face
designed exclusively for Hallmark by Hermann Zapf.
The paper is Hallclear, White Imitation Parchment
and Ivory Fiesta Parchment. The cover is bound
with natural weave book cloth and Torino paper.

This book was designed and illustrated by Pavel Wawr...
The artist's unique style is the result of
experimentation and techniques of silk screen printing.
The typeface is Missouri, set in eight point ... graphic are
designed and produced ... reproduced by Herman ... set
... page ... in Italian, in ... the same ... in ivory ... Paris ...
and ivory finish Paris ... The cover is bound
with a ... text book cloth and Torino paper